BIRDS

A Piccolo Factbook

Contents

BIRDS

By David Lambert

Editor: Jacqui Bailey

Series Design: David Jefferis

A Piccolo Factbook

How Birds Live

Birds are among the most successful animals alive. There are about 9000 kinds of bird alive today, compared with only about 4000 kinds of mammal. Like the mammals, the birds are warm blooded. Therefore, unlike fish or reptiles, most birds can stay active even in cold weather. Feathers help to keep their bodies warm, and feathered wings help many birds to fly about to find food and escape danger. A bird's beak and claws make useful tools and weapons.

Birds come in many sizes, shapes and colours. But each species is specially built for the kind of life it leads.

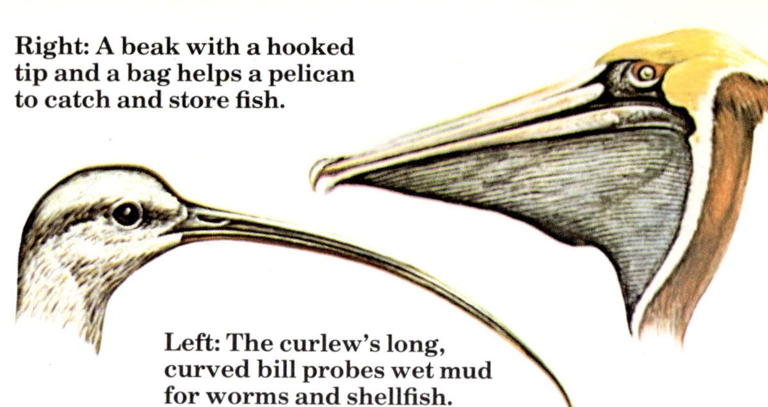

Right: A beak with a hooked tip and a bag helps a pelican to catch and store fish.

Left: The curlew's long, curved bill probes wet mud for worms and shellfish.

Feeding

Birds use wings or feet to fly or walk in search of food. But most seize and hold food in their beaks. Many a beak can also break or tear up food. The shape of a bird's beak is a clue to the kind of food that the bird eats.

Beak Shapes
Herons and other fish-eaters have long, pointed beaks for seizing fish. Bee-eaters catch bees and dragonflies in their long, slim beaks. Swifts have short beaks with mouths that gape wide to trap insects in the air. A finch's strong, stubby beak can crack seeds open. To split an olive stone,

Below: The hawk's hooked beak tears its prey apart.

Above: The cardinal uses its sturdy beak for cracking open hard seeds.

Below: A merganser's saw-edged beak grips fish.

Above: The toucan's big beak plucks fruit from twigs too thin to perch on.

a hawfinch exerts a force 1500 times greater than its own weight. Owls and eagles have a strong, hooked beak to tear up meat. A swan's broad beak grasps and pulls up plants.

Gizzards and Crops

Birds have no teeth for chewing food. Instead, many swallow grit. Inside a stomach called a gizzard, grit grinds swallowed food into pieces small enough to be digested. A bag called a crop bulges from a bird's lower throat. The crop stores extra food when the gizzard is full. A bird can fill its crop with food, then fly somewhere safe to digest it.

Below: A kingfisher's long, sharp beak is ideal for grasping fish it has plucked from the water surface.

Above: Woodpeckers' sharp bills drill holes in trees to reach insects.

Feather Care

A bird's feathers play a vital part in its way of life. Untidy feathers can make flying difficult. Dirty feathers let body heat leak away. Parasites among the feathers harm a bird's health. So feather care is important to birds. But one kind of swan has 25,000 feathers, and even a tiny hummingbird has almost 1000. So it is not surprising

Below: You can make a birdbath with an old dustbin lid propped up on bricks. Birds will enjoy splashing in it.

Above: Birds preen each other as well as themselves. This helps to keep a group of birds friendly.

that birds spend much of their lives simply keeping themselves clean.

Preening
Birds largely keep their feathers clean by preening. With its beak, a bird takes oil from a preen gland near its tail. The bird then runs its beak over its feathers. This oils the feathers and makes them waterproof. (Ducks that lose the oil from their feathers may sink instead of floating.) Preening also smooths ruffled feathers and removes dirt, and parasites like fleas and lice.

Anting
Many kinds of perching bird place ants on their feathers. Ants produce a chemical called formic acid. It is thought that this acid helps the birds in some way, possibly by killing mites: small parasites that live among the feathers.

Bathing
Land birds splash in puddles or beat their wings in dust. Water birds plunge under water. Then both groups preen. Bathing and preening help to keep feathers clean.

Moulting
Cleaning feathers does not stop them wearing out. At least once a year most birds moult: they shed old feathers and grow new ones. Birds moult before winter. By then new feathers will have grown to keep them warm.

Below: As the wings flap down they push the bird up and forward.

A flying bird draws its wings to full upstroke.

Flying

To fly through air a bird needs a lighter and more powerful body than other animals of the same size that only walk or swim.

Bones and Feathers

A bird's bones weigh very little, for they are mostly thin and hollow. But struts inside them make them strong. The thin skull holds big, keen eyes and a brain that delicately controls how the bird moves and balances.

The wings and tail as well as the bones are light, for they are mostly made of feathers.

Muscle Power

Weight for weight, a bird is far stronger than a man. Big, powerful muscles joined to the wings and breastbone flap the wings up and down.

Muscles get energy from oxygen and sugar. These are pumped in the blood to the muscles by a big, fast-beating heart. The sugar comes from food. The oxygen comes from breathed-in air. When a bird breathes air into its lungs, some air is stored in other hollows in the body. As a bird breathes out, this extra air flows through the lungs. So some oxygen is always entering a bird's blood as it flies. This keeps its muscles working.

Below: Small birds can launch themselves into the air with one leap. Large birds need a running take-off.

Above: The feathers open to let air through as the wings rise.

Wings

A bird's wings are made of feathers growing from the equivalent of our arm, wrist and finger bones. If it loses a few feathers from its wings a bird can still fly.

As a bird flaps its wings, the tips twist around to thrust air backward. This forces the bird forward.

As the wings move forward they keep the bird in the air. For a wing's upper side is curved and its lower side is flattish. This makes air rush faster over a wing than under it. The air above is thinned out and the wing is sucked up into the thin air and pushed up by the thicker air below. This gives the bird *lift*.

Small wings give a fast-flying bird as much lift as large wings give a slowly flying bird of the same size.

A pheasant's broad, short wings help it to fly up steeply in a wood. Swifts fly fast and nimbly on slim, curved wings. Eagles soar on warm, rising air without flapping their broad, long wings. In a similar way, seagulls use their long, narrow wings to glide on the winds blowing over the sea.

Migrating

In summer millions of birds feed and breed in northern lands. When autumn comes, food grows extremely scarce there. To find enough to eat many birds migrate. Almost half of all the birds that breed in Europe fly south to Africa to spend the winter there. In some years as many as 3000 million birds journey south, across or around the Mediterranean Sea. In most autumns it is as though 300,000 birds passed over every kilometre of North Africa's long, long coast.

Each autumn many millions of birds also fly south from North America to the warm, sunny lands of Central and South America.

Incredible Journeys
Some birds migrate much farther than others. From

In the spring these four kinds of bird all fly back to Europe after spending the winter in Africa.

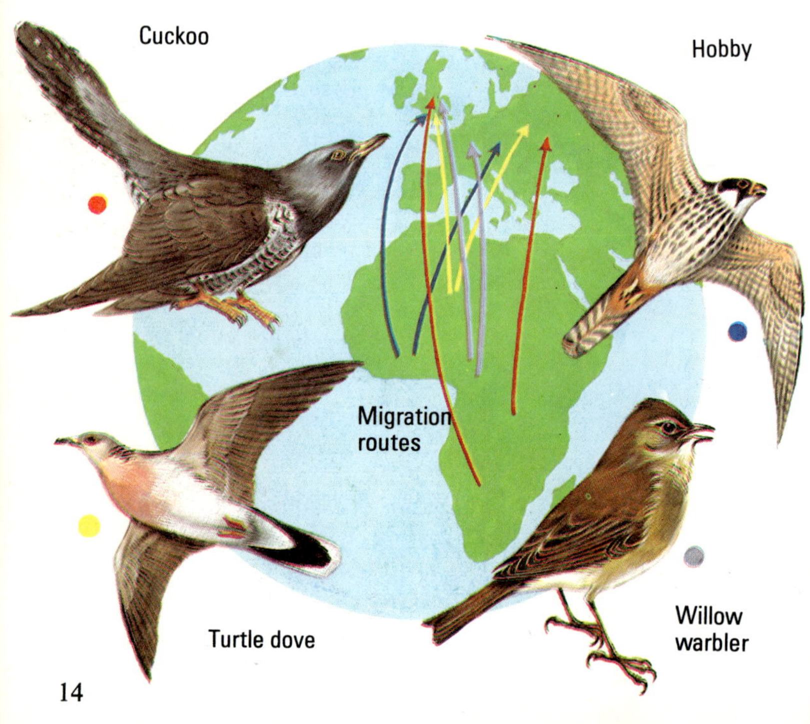

Scandinavia, chaffinches cross a mere few hundred kilometres of sea to winter in the British Isles. But swallows fly as many as 9000 kilometres to reach southern Africa. Some Arctic terns fly nearly 13,000 kilometres to Antarctica, then back again next spring. No other birds migrate that far.

Greenland wheatears make the longest non-stop flight of any land bird that migrates. These small birds fly 3000 kilometres non-stop from Greenland to Spain.

Fuel for Flight

Some migrants feed on the way. Others get their energy by storing food as body fat before they start. A warbler may double its weight before setting off across a sea or desert, or both.

If headwinds slow it down, the bird may have to fly three days and nights without stopping to take a rest.

These four birds breed in the far north. Then they fly south to spend the winter in Europe.

How Birds Breed

Before a hen bird can lay fertile eggs from which young birds can hatch, she must meet and mate with a cock bird of her own kind. In many species the meeting takes place on a piece of land where the pair will raise and feed its family. This area is a bird's territory. A golden eagle's territory may cover several square kilometres. A robin's territory is just a garden.

Claiming Territory

In most species, males claim territories before they meet their mates. Males have various ways of staking out their claims. Drab birds like nightingales sing loudly. Brightly coloured birds like stonechats flaunt themselves from perches where other birds can clearly see them. A male may take no notice of males of other species. But it will threaten invading males of its own kind. Robins fight fiercely enough to maim or even kill.

Cock birds of paradise and a cock bower bird (centre). Their colours help to attract mates.

Winning a Mate

When a female bird of his own kind appears, a male tries to win her. Brightly coloured males like peacocks, pheasants and birds of paradise display their brilliant plumage. Bower birds build little avenues and may gather brightly coloured stones to decorate them.

Different species of birds have different ways of winning a mate. Buntings take special courtship flights. Some drakes perform a kind of nodding dance. Grebes and divers have special courting cries. Pretending to drink or preen in one another's company brings some pairs together. A male Adélie penguin gives a female a stone. If she takes it, both build a pebble nest.

Courtship bonds a pair together and helps each bird to overcome its instinct to drive the other off. After courting, most birds mate on land. But ducks and swans mate in the water, and swifts pair in the air.

Building Nests

Once birds have paired they build a nest where the hen can lay and hatch her eggs in safety.

Birds often build with bits of grass, twigs, wool or mud. Some are extremely clever builders. Weaver birds use their beaks to knot grasses together. Oven birds make domed nests of mud. One hummingbird uses downy plant fibres bound with spiders' webs.

Most birds hide their nests from enemies in bushes, trees or grass. But woodpeckers peck nesting holes in rotting trees. Sand martins, bee-eaters and kingfishers nest in holes in banks. A kingfisher lays her eggs on a pile of smelly fishbones at the far end of her hole.

Unusual Nurseries

Some nests are very strange indeed. The African palm swift uses saliva to glue a pad of feathers to a drooping palm leaf. Then she glues her eggs to the pad to stop them falling off. The fairy tern builds no nest at all; instead she balances her single egg on a bare branch.

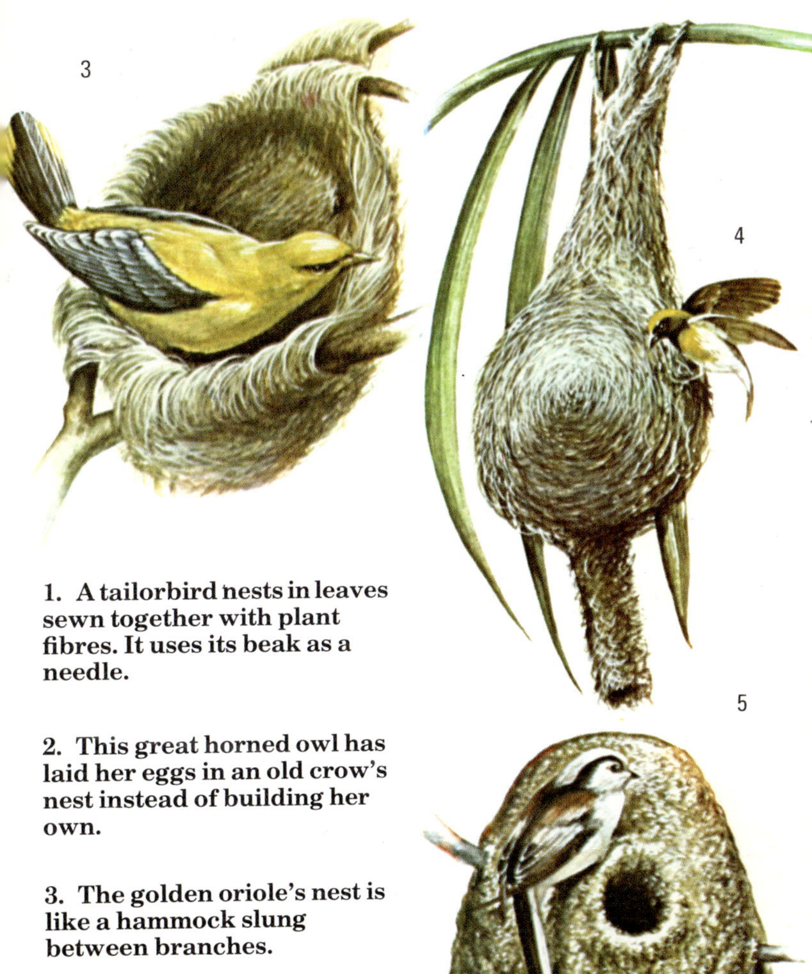

1. A tailorbird nests in leaves sewn together with plant fibres. It uses its beak as a needle.

2. This great horned owl has laid her eggs in an old crow's nest instead of building her own.

3. The golden oriole's nest is like a hammock slung between branches.

4. The baya weaver has a nest with a funnel leading to the middle where the eggs are laid.

5. The long-tailed tit's nest is a hollow ball with a hole in the side.

Eggs

Birds' eggs are packages that nourish and protect *embryos* – baby birds that grow inside. Each egg yolk provides food for an embryo. Each shell helps to prevent an embryo from drying up.

Egg Facts
The long-lived gannet lays one egg a year. The short-lived pheasant may lay 17 eggs.

Eggs come in many sizes. The ostrich lays the largest eggs. An ostrich egg is as big as 24 hens' eggs. It may weigh 3500 times more than a Helena's hummingbird egg, the world's smallest.

Some eggs have unusual shapes. A guillemot's egg looks like a pear. If it is pushed, it simply rolls in a

Birds' eggs come in many sizes and colours (left). Compare the difference in size of a hummingbird egg with that of an ostrich (below).

Hummingbird egg

Ostrich egg

circle. Its shape helps to stop it falling off the rock ledge where it was laid.

Eggs laid in the open may be coloured in ways that hide them from enemies. But eggs that are laid in dark holes are often white.

Incubating Eggs

To hatch their eggs birds must somehow keep them warm. They usually sit on their eggs. If the female sits, her mate may feed her. In some species both parents sit, and sometimes hatching the eggs is left entirely to the male.

Hatching times vary. The great spotted woodpecker's eggs take only 10 days to hatch. Wandering albatrosses' eggs take 80 days.

Woodcocks' eggs have brown and grey markings. This makes it difficult for enemies to see them on the woodland floor.

A mallee fowl's eggs are hatched by heat from rotting leaves in a mound of leaves and sand.

Raising Young

After weeks developing inside an egg, a baby bird is ready to come out. It takes its first breath from the air stored in the fat end of the egg. Then it chips away the shell with help from its egg-tooth. This is a hard knob at the tip of its beak.

Some chicks can run, swim, and even partly feed themselves as soon as they have left the egg. Chickens, partridges and ducks all start life like this. But most eggs laid in holes or complicated nests hatch into chicks that are naked, blind and helpless. Such chicks need a lot of care.

Food for Life

Many baby birds eat insect food. In 18 days a pair of blue tits may bring 10,000 caterpillars to their hungry brood of 10 chicks.

Seabirds tend to feed their chicks on fish. Some pelicans fly 160 kilometres every day to find fish for their young. Pigeons feed their chicks on 'pigeons' milk', a cheesy substance made from the lining of the parent's crop.

Baby coots swim from their floating nest soon after they hatch. But the parents guard them.

Blackbirds poke worms into their waiting babies' mouths. But a herring gull's chick must peck at the red spot on its parent's beak to make it bring up food.

Nestlings produce body waste as white packets which the parents soon remove. Otherwise predators might see their nest and eat the helpless chicks inside.

Protective Parents

Besides feeding and cleaning their chicks, parents help to protect them. A parent bird will spread its feathers over her chicks to guard them from hot sunshine or pouring rain.

If a fox draws near her nest, a lapwing may try to lure the enemy away. She flops along the ground as though she has a broken wing. If a man walks through a colony of terns or skuas, the birds will swoop around his head until they drive him off.

When the young birds are ready they will leave the nest. Young razorbills tumble off cliff ledges into the sea at 17 days old, too young to fly. But a wandering albatross is nine months old before it leaves home.

Birds in the Trees

Trees offer birds safety from enemies that cannot climb or fly. Forest and woodland birds can build their nests high up, or hidden among leaves, or inside hollow trees. Then, too, some kinds of wood and forest are rich in the buds, leaves, seeds or insects that woodland birds, like those shown here, are built to find and eat.

The Perching Birds

Only certain kinds of bird are well suited to a woodland life. Most belong to the large group of perching birds. Three in every five kinds of bird alive today are perching birds. A perching bird has three forward-pointing toes and one backward-pointing toe on each foot. This toe arrangement helps both feet to grip a twig or branch. So perching birds are well designed to spend their lives among the trees and feed on the plentiful food there.

Many perching birds live in woods of oak, ash, beech or other deciduous trees that shed leaves in autumn.

Eating Buds and Seeds

The buds and seeds of Europe's deciduous woods feed such strong-beaked perching birds as greenfinches, bullfinches and hawfinches. In early spring, finches feed on buds. In summer they catch insects for their young. In autumn and winter there are plenty of seeds for them to eat.

The Insect-Eaters

Each spring, the soft new leaves yield food for millions of insects. At this time of year, many insect-eating birds fly from Africa to Europe's deciduous woodlands to feed and to raise their families.

The migrants include many warblers. These tend to be small, brownish birds that look alike and hide among the leaves. But each kind has a special song. Males sing to attract mates and warn rival males to stay away. Willow warblers and chiff-chaffs are warblers that often share a wood. Both eat similar kinds of insect. But chiff-chaffs feed high up and willow warblers feed low down. So each kind leaves food for the other.

In autumn, insects die off and most of Europe's insect-eating birds migrate. But tits and tree-creepers stay on.

Their sharp beaks find insect eggs and pupae hidden in cracks in tree bark.

Birds of Both Continents

Some birds living in North America's deciduous woodlands are similar to those of Europe. In both continents, swallows swoop above the trees. Their open mouths act like nets to capture insects. Tree-creepers and woodpeckers work their way up tree trunks. Both have long, stiff tail feathers that act as props to help them climb. Wrens creep about like mice in shrubs and on the woodland floor. Jays hop about at every level in their search for food. In autumn and winter jays largely feed upon acorns, which they find and store for future use. In spring these big, bold birds steal the eggs and chicks of woodland birds smaller and weaker than themselves. Hawks hunt small birds in American and European woods.

The brown wrens and tree-creepers of an American wood look much like their European cousins. But the North American blue jay is unmistakable.

Tree-creepers

Coniferous Woodland

The world's great northern forests of cone-bearing, evergreen trees are not rich in juicy buds, leaves and insects. Nuthatches and tree-creepers like those shown here often live in mixed woods. But coniferous woods lack the nuts that nuthatches eat and

may have too few insects to satisfy tree-creepers.

Needle-shaped conifer leaves taste unpleasantly of sticky resin. Resin tends to stop dead leaves from rotting into food for tiny animals and grubs. The forest floor is bare, and snow lies thickly on the ground in the long, cold winters. So fewer kinds of bird can feed and breed here. Crossbills are among the smaller birds that do.

Crossbill and Capercaillie

Crossbills use their beaks to cut cones off the conifers. The crossed tips of a crossbill's beak help it to free the seeds inside.

Capercaillies are among the few northern forest birds that feed on leaves. These big, dark birds largely eat the shoots and buds of spruce trees. Capercaillies spend the summer on the forest floor, but perch on trees in winter.

Winged Hunters

Long-eared owls hunt in northern woods at night. Their soft feathers make no sound and their large eyes and ears help them to find the small birds and mammals that they prey on. Like all owls, long-eared owls have sharp, hooked beaks for tearing flesh.

Owls, crossbills and capercaillies all have ways of finding food in the great northern forests.

Tropical Forests

The steamy rain forests of the tropics hold more kinds of bird than anywhere else. Because it is always warm and moist, there are always trees with leaves, flowers and fruits for plant-eating birds to eat. Then, too, there are always billions of insects for the insect-eaters. Both those groups of bird in turn provide meals for eagles, owls and other birds of prey.

Different kinds of bird find food in each of the three main levels of the forest.

The Forest Floor
The forest floor is dark and dim. In Asian forests, jungle fowl and pheasants hunt among the rotting leaves for seeds and insects. In Africa, guinea fowl scratch for bulbs and snails. The forest floor in South America is home to tinamous – birds that very seldom fly, and look rather like partridges.

Parakeets, touracos and hornbills are all found in Old World forests. Touracos live in Africa. Parakeets and hornbills live in Africa and Asia.

The Middle Layer
The second forest layer rises from the forest floor. Huge tree trunks soar upward. Climbing plants with stems like ropes cling to the trees and hang in loops.

Small insect-eating birds flit between the trees in the dim light. Many birds of several kinds roam together through a forest. In Asia, shamas and trogons hunt low down, flycatchers and babblers fly above them, and minivets and white-eyes fly even higher.

In the same way armies of small birds travel through the middle layer of African and South American forests.

But some of the largest and smallest birds thrive at the highest forest level.

Ring-necked parakeet

Hornbills
Touraco

Macaw

Life in the Treetops

If you look down on a tropical rain forest from a plane you see a green sea made up of the leaves of closely packed treetops. Only the very tallest trees rise above this canopy. Where they reach the light, brightly coloured flowers bloom and produce fruits that ripen.

Many of the forest birds hide and feed up here. Most kinds are brightly coloured, and some are built in ways that help them to eat special kinds of food.

The hummingbirds of South America have long, slim beaks for sipping nectar from the forest flowers. While it feeds, a hummingbird hovers like a tiny helicopter. Its wings may beat 80 times each second. Some hummingbirds are the smallest birds

on Earth. One, the Helena's, is lighter than a large moth.

Macaws and other members of the parrot family have beaks strong enough for cracking nuts. A parrot's beak is also useful as an extra 'hand' for climbing.

The toucans of South America and the hornbills of Africa and Asia have huge, awkward-looking beaks. These help the birds to reach fruits hanging from twigs too light for them to perch on.

Above the Trees

Winged hunters speed or soar above the forest canopy. Swifts whizz about in search of insects. In South-East Asia, a falconet little larger than a sparrow hunts small birds. The harpy eagle of South America swoops down to seize sloths and monkeys.

Water Birds

Many ducks, swans, geese and other birds feed in and breed on fresh water. Ducks, geese and swans have broad beaks that help them to pull up or tear off mouthfuls of water plants or grasses. Some have beaks with a hooked tip useful for digging out seeds that have fallen in the mud. Mallard and teal are ducks that also sieve water through their beaks to find snails.

Different kinds of bird that live near one another feed on different foods. Shoveller ducks sieve food from the surface of the water. But pintails upend and find food under the water.

The Fish-Eaters

Some freshwater birds live on fish. Most of these birds have sharp beaks for seizing prey. Kingfishers dive like hawks. Herons ambush fish near the water's edge. Grebes and divers hunt by swimming under water. The long-necked tropical birds called darters use their long beaks as fishing spears.

Female swan with cygnets

Swimming and Wading

Ducks, swans, geese and divers swim by using their webbed feet as paddles. But not all water birds swim. The long-legged heron only wades. Lily trotters run about on floating water lilies. These small birds from the tropics have long, slim toes that help to spread their weight so they do not sink.

Baby Water Birds

Moorhens, coots, grebes and swans tend to build floating nests, half hidden among reeds. This helps to protect them from enemies that live on land. Their newly-hatched babies can soon swim. But grebe chicks and cygnets (baby swans) sometimes climb aboard their mother's back. This protects them from fishes like pike and catfish that eat many baby water birds.

Beach and Mudflat

In winter, spring or autumn thousands of long-legged wading birds patrol the low shores of northern Europe.

The surface of the sand or mud may seem quite bare and empty. But underneath live millions of small molluscs, worms, shrimps and other tiny seashore creatures. These are the food the wading birds are hunting.

Short Beaks

Various kinds of wading bird are able to find and eat different sorts of food. The small, stocky ringed plover runs and pauses as if it senses food beneath the mud. Then it quickly dips its head and plucks a laver spire snail from the mud. The plover's beak is shorter than waders' beaks, but it can reach spire snails because these do not burrow deeply.

The sanderling also has a fairly short beak, yet it can reach cockles because these

tubby shellfish also live close to the surface. But sanderlings, dunlins and sandpipers largely feed on sandhoppers: small relatives of shrimps and crabs. Sanderlings race along sandy beaches, just ahead of the waves.

Knots are wading birds with beaks long enough to probe the mud for a kind of sandhopper that burrows fairly deeply. Knots and dunlins also feast on the seaweed-fly maggots found in heaps of rotting seaweed washed high up on the beach.

Long Beaks

Only waders with long beaks can reach worms and molluscs that burrow really deeply. Redshanks can dig out bivalve (two-shelled) molluscs called tellins. Curlews have long, downcurved beaks that can reach all but the very deepest burrowers. Nerves in the tip of a curlew's beak feel nearby movement in the sand and so help the bird to find its prey.

Strange Beaks

Some waders have very strange beaks, shaped for feeding on special kinds of seaside food. For instance, New Zealand's wrybilled plover has a beak that bends to the right. This bird finds food by slipping its beak beneath stones as it walks around them.

Perhaps the strangest beaks belong to birds that feed in the shallow waters of lagoons behind a beach.

The avocet scythes its long, upcurved beak from side to side to capture shrimps and insects. The spoonbill hunts small animals in the same way, with a beak shaped like two flat spoons. The flamingo takes in water; then squirts it through its strangely bent beak, trapping food particles on the hairs inside.

Rocky Shores

For some birds rocky shores provide a well-stocked larder. For others, the cliffs above the rocks are both safe roosting places and nurseries.

Among the Rocks

Some wading birds feed on shellfish, worms and other creatures living among rocks covered daily by the tide. The oystercatcher is well designed for eating mussels. Its beak has a flat, sharp end like a chisel. An oystercatcher breaks open a closed mussel shell by hammering it with its beak. If the shell is already open, the bird slips its beak between the shell halves and cuts the muscle that closes them. Then it chisels the flesh from the shell.

On the Cliffs

Some seabirds lay eggs and raise their chicks on ledges half way up sea cliffs. Here the young seabirds are safe from the foxes, cats and rats that destroy many of the young of birds that nest on level ground inland.

Each female guillemot lays her single egg on bare rock in the open. A razorbill prefers to hide her egg in a crevice under a rock. Cormorants lay their eggs in bulky seaweed nests. Puffins usually nest in the safety of burrows on the grassy slopes above the sea cliffs.

Some seabird colonies are vast. One single Greenland colony holds two million guillemots. So many seabirds can nest close together because they can all find enough food by fishing in the sea.

Guillemot
Shag
Razorbill
Puffin

Gulls and Terns

Gulls are seabirds familiar to almost anyone who has visited the sea. These big pale creatures use their long, strong wings to fly and glide easily above the waves.

There are many kinds of gull. Herring gulls are the ones most often seen on the shore. These birds are as big as a chicken, but their appetites are more like those of eagles and vultures. Herring gulls use their powerful beaks to tear flesh from dead fish or other creatures washed up on the shore. They will stamp upon a sandy beach to scare worms to the surface. Then they eat the worms. Herring gulls will also kill and eat young rabbits and young terns. In places where the gulls threaten nesting terns people may poison them or prick their eggs to stop them hatching. Otherwise herring gulls have very few enemies and can live 20 years.

A common gull catches a crab. Common gulls look like herring gulls, but fly inland more often.

Unlike a common tern, an Arctic tern has a red beak with no black tip.

Sea Swallows

At first glance, most types of tern look like slim, black-headed gulls as they fly above the waves. But terns have narrow, pointed wings and long, forked tails like swallows.

Common terns and Arctic terns fly north to Europe for the summer months, to breed.

People often see them flying up and down offshore along the coast. To find food a tern hovers and gazes down into the water. When it sees a fish just below the surface, the bird dives and plunges partly under water. Then it flies up with its prey grasped in its bill.

A male common tern bows and scrapes to his mate on the ground, or displays himself by flying with a fish grasped in his beak.

The female lays her eggs in a hollow in the ground behind a beach. A colony of terns will dive bomb any enemy that comes too near to their eggs. The terns may use their sharp beaks to stab to death young rabbits that stray close to their nests.

Albatrosses

Most seabirds seldom stray very far from land. But albatrosses spend most of their lives on the open ocean. These birds have short legs but long, narrow wings. The outstretched wings of a wandering albatross are as long as two tall men lying end to end. No other bird on Earth has wings as long as that.

Most kinds of albatross prefer the stormy oceans of the far south. The birds glide above the waves for hours with hardly any wing movement. They feed by plucking squid or other small creatures from the sea.

Albatrosses only land to breed. It can take nearly a year before an egg becomes a chick old enough to fly. Large albatrosses breed only every other year.

These big birds are long lived. Probably only three in every 100 die each year. An albatross is likely to live to over 30 – longer than almost any other wild bird.

Albatrosses (centre) are at home on windy oceans. An albatross can glide for weeks on the winds that blow across the troughs and crests of waves. The bird turns into the wind to climb and then swoops downwind to pick up speed for its next turn into the wind. An albatross steers with its feet, which stick out well beyond its short tail. The other seabirds give some idea of the huge wingspan of the albatross.

Open Countryside

Moors and heaths, mountains, Arctic lands, and the hot and cool grasslands – each kind of open countryside has a special set of birds that breed and feed there.

Moors and Heaths

Shoots, seeds and insects provide food for the smaller birds that live among the bracken, gorse and heather. Bilberries, crowberries and earthworms are favourite foods of the ring ouzel – a

Left: Buzzards can be seen over moors, fields and woods.

Below: Ring ouzels go south to escape winter.

relative of the blackbird. If danger threatens, a ring ouzel quickly dodges behind a moorland rock.

Dippers catch the insect larvae that live in fast-flowing hill streams.

In some parts of Europe, great grey shrikes perch on lonely trees and swoop on insects and little birds like siskins and skylarks.

Buzzards are broad-winged birds of prey, related to the eagles. They soar in circles in the air above moors and forests. Buzzards feed on animals as small as beetles or as large as rabbits.

Above: A great grey shrike. Some shrikes hang dead prey on thorn trees, but often they forget these 'larders'.

Below: Dippers plunge into streams and swim with their wings as they hunt for food.

Right: The Andean condor has a wingspan as wide as two small cars. It soars over mountain peaks and eats dead animals.

Right: Ravens are the world's largest crows. They nest on mountain cliffs, and will tumble and dive playfully in mid-air.

Mountain Birds

Steep slopes, fierce winds, and cold, thin air make life hard among the world's high mountains. Few mammals live higher than trees can grow. Yet some birds thrive. For birds have special breathing systems. They can hold air in their hollow bones as well as in their lungs. Then, too, a bird's heart pumps blood fast around the body to keep it working. Feathers help to keep birds warm in the chilly winds. Lastly, dark colours protect crows and eagles from harmful rays which reach mountain tops from the Sun.

Mountain Meals

Somehow mountain birds find food. Some feed on seeds or insects blown higher up the slopes than plants can grow. Alpine choughs walk about in search of worms and insects. These sharp-billed crows have been seen near the top of Mount Everest, the highest peak on Earth. Big birds of prey may fly higher still. Eagles and vultures soar on rising air currents to scan the ground for small mammals or dead animals. Big kites called lammergeiers drop bones from a height to crack them. Then they eat the soft marrow inside.

Small birds cannot fly against strong mountain winds. Instead these birds stay near the ground. A wallcreeper probing for insects can climb head-first down a cliff.

Birds of Arctic Lands

From May to September the far north teems with breeding birds. Millions fly there in May to raise their families. For in the summer months northern marshes and shrubby areas brim with plant and insect foods. But in September, frost kills off many plants and insects. Then most of the birds must fly south with their young before the long, cold Arctic winter truly starts.

Summer Visitors

Most of the Arctic's summer visitors are water birds. Seabirds crowd the coastal cliffs. Terns nest here and there on sandy shores. Ducks, geese, swans, and waders breed in bogs or marshes, or by pools and rivers. Among the water birds are divers that can plunge 70 metres deep, but need a 36-metre take-off from the water. Here, too, breed whooper swans almost as heavy as a four-year-old child. Few other birds so heavy can lift into the air.

Stay-at-Homes

Only hardy birds that can stand cold and find food in an Arctic winter live all year in the far north.

Snow buntings have been seen near the North Pole. No other songbirds fly so far north. For their size, these little birds have a large surface to lose heat from. But feathers help to keep them warm and the seeds they eat are very nourishing.

On snowy ground, white feathers hide snow buntings, ptarmigan, and snowy owls from Arctic enemies. Few other birds can winter in the far north.

The ptarmigan has feathered legs that help to stop it losing body heat. When snow hides the plants they feed on, ptarmigan fly off to hills swept bare of snow by wind. Here, though, these meaty birds are hunted by gyrfalcons. Gyrfalcons hunt farther north than any other birds of prey.

Snowy owls also roam the Arctic all year round. By day or night they hunt the small, mouse-like lemmings. A family of snowy owls eats up to 80 lemmings a day. When lemmings are scarce, snowy owls fly south to feed outside the Arctic.

Meadow Birds

Meadows are grazing lands for cows and sheep. They are often made by draining swamps and cutting down forests. Meadowland offers some kinds of wild bird plenty of food, and many of these birds have come to flourish in these areas.

Lapwings once lived mainly on the edges of marshes. Now many feed and nest on grassland. Lapwings eat worms, slugs, snails and insects.

Partridges used to be found on moors and sand dunes. Now they chiefly feed in fields, on clover, grass and insects. When feeding partridges see someone coming, they crouch down until they are almost trodden on. Then they spring into the air and fly away fast and low with loudly whirring wings.

Pheasants, rooks and woodpigeons often feed in fields but nest in woods. Pheasants are big and strong enough to scratch away winter snow, to find seeds or grass to eat.

Soaring Songsters

Skylarks were once mostly moorland birds. Now you often hear one singing as it flutters high above a meadow. A skylark's song may last minutes – longer than almost any other birdsong.

Skylarks largely eat grass. If snow hides the grass they are too weak to scratch the snow away, and starve unless they fly away.

Like the other meadow birds that we have mentioned, skylarks build their nests upon the ground.

Above: A skylark's nest is hidden only by the blades of grass around it.

Left: Four kinds of bird that feed in meadows. Pheasants and partridges always live in the same piece of countryside. But some quails and lapwings migrate. Migrating quails used to be so plentiful that people on one tiny islet caught 160,000 a year.

Birds of Wild Grasslands

Wild grasslands cover huge parts of the world too dry for trees. Short grasses make up prairie, steppe and pampas lands found in countries with cold winters. Tall grasses make up the hot, tropical savanna grasslands.

Grass itself yields food for many grassland birds. Doves, larks and weaver birds, related to sparrows, feed on grass seeds. Billions of insects are gobbled up by savanna birds like bee-eaters, guinea fowl, ostriches and bustards.

Eagles and falcons hunt the plant-eaters and seed-eaters. Marabou storks and vultures soar above the African savanna looking for dead animals. Their keen eyes can spot corpses far below.

Grassland Heavyweights

To avoid their enemies many birds nest, and hide or run, among the grasses. Africa's vulturine guinea fowl, kori bustard and ostrich all have long, strong legs for running. Some running birds are very large. A kori bustard stands as high as a man's shoulder and weighs as much as a five-year-old child. It may be the heaviest bird able to fly. An ostrich is much larger, but it is too heavy to take off.

Four kinds of bird seen on Africa's savanna grasslands. Bee-eaters eat insects and nest in holes in soft cliffs. Oxpeckers eat ticks that bore into the skins of buffaloes and other big beasts. Ostriches eat plants and small animals. Secretary birds are long-legged hawks. Unlike any other hawk they hunt on the ground. Snakes are a favourite prey.

Five birds often seen in or near a garden. Blue tits hunt insects on shrubs and trees. Song thrushes eat worms on lawns. Goldfinches feed on thistle seeds. House sparrows nest on houses and swallows often nest in garden sheds.

Town Birds

Towns and gardens provide food, shelter and nest sites for many birds that lived in other places before people learnt to build. Most kinds of bird came from the forest edge.

In London and some other cities, huge flocks of starlings fly in every night to roost on ledges high above the ground. Here, too, town pigeons nest. For them buildings are just man-made cliffs, much like the natural cliffs where their wild relatives the rock doves nest. Town pigeons, starlings and house sparrows all eat food scraps dropped on city streets.

Parks and gardens are larders for several groups of birds. Here, thrushes find worms. Tits catch insects. Finches of various kinds feed on weed seeds. On lakes in city parks wild ducks fly down to feed with tame ones.

A Bird that Needs People
Almost all the birds seen in towns and gardens can live in other places. Only the house crow of southern Asia seems to scrounge all its food from towns or villages.

Unusual Visitors

Sparrows or starlings live in many cities of the world. But in some cities, towns and villages you find more unusual kinds of bird.

Chimney Swifts

Migrating chimney swifts

Chimney swifts

visit towns in North America. In late evening thousands of these birds fly twittering around big, unused factory chimneys. As darkness falls, the flock swoops down to sleep in the chimney (left).

Before people built chimneys in North America, chimney swifts used hollow trees.

A white stork's nest is a big untidy bundle of sticks. Some villages may have a lot of nests.

White Storks

White storks are even stranger summer visitors in certain towns. These large, long-legged birds wade in streams and marshes to hunt for frogs and fish. But white storks nest among the roof-tops of some European towns and villages. Villagers who think that storks bring luck raise platforms on their roofs especially for storks to build their large untidy nests on.

Before people made houses, white storks used to nest on cliffs and trees.

Strange Nesting Places

Several kinds of bird that usually nest in the country sometimes nest in towns. In Moscow, rooks built nests on platforms high up on poles that held the lights that shone down on a sports stadium.

In several cities wood-pigeons have built nests on builders' scaffolding.

Kestrels are small falcons that nest on office buildings in the middle of London. They hunt mice and sparrows. There is a plan to free captive peregrine falcons to nest on New York skyscrapers and hunt the city pigeons. In winter waders may be seen in sewage farms, which have much in common with their usual mud-flats.

In the Garden

It can be fun watching birds in a garden. A good way is to leave them food where you can see it from a window, and cats cannot reach it.

Put out kitchen scraps like bits of bread, cheese, bacon rind and cooked potato. You can buy mixed birdseed for seed-eating birds. Tits enjoy coconut, peanuts and fat. The more kinds of food you offer the more kinds of bird you may attract.

Greedy birds may drive the others away, so use several feeding places if they do.

Also put out some water in a shallow dish for birds to drink and bathe in.

Feeding birds matters most in winter when food is hard to find. The birds may soon depend on you for food. So keep feeding them all through the winter months.

Nesting Boxes
In autumn or winter fix a few nest-boxes high up on walls or trees around your home. Put the boxes out of reach of cats and strong sunshine. Next spring birds may use the boxes as homes for raising families.

Hang coconut and peanuts like this. But never give birds salted peanuts or desiccated coconut as these can be harmful.

Two kinds of bird table. The one above hangs from a tree. The other table is screwed to the top of a post fixed in the ground. Each table is made of a thick piece of marine plywood with strips of wood screwed on around the edges. If you make a table like one of these, paint the wood with a preservative to stop it rotting. Let the preservative dry for at least 48 hours, so it does not harm the birds.

Studying Birds

Most of us like to know the names of birds we see or hear in town and country.

To identify a strange bird write down the special things about it. Put how big it is compared with some bird you know. Describe its beak, legs, wings and tail. If it has special colours, try to sketch the bird and mark them on your sketch.

Notice where you see the bird and how it is behaving. Perhaps it is perching in a tree, hopping in a park, walking on a beach, or swimming. It may be flying in a straight line or a looping line. Some kinds of bird soar and others glide.

All these things are easier to see if you can watch birds

Sparrowhawk pellet

Crow pellet

Heron pellet

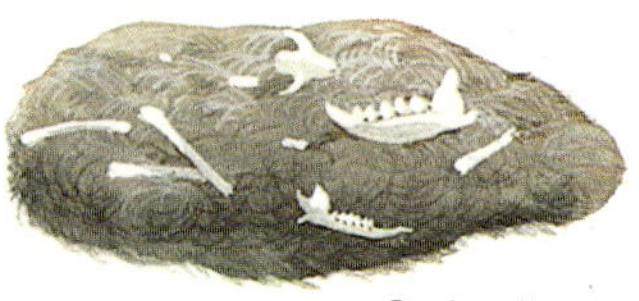

Owl pellet

Birds cough up pellets of undigested food. These pellets show what the bird has eaten. You can often find pellets below an owl's resting place. Look at the ground near a post, tree or ruined building.

You can recognize many flying birds by their shapes even when you cannot see their colours.

through binoculars. Their lenses make far-off birds seem near and clear.

If you hear an unusual bird song or call, try to describe this too.

Always write your bird notes on the spot, while you can still exactly remember what you saw or heard.

Tracks and Traces
Birds leave footprints in snow and mud. They drop feathers and cough up pellets containing bits of undigested food. Some peck holes in fruits and nuts. Many build special kinds of nest.

Books called field guides help you identify birds and their tracks and traces.

Use tweezers to pull a pellet apart to discover its ingredients. An owl pellet may hold vole and shrew fur and bones.

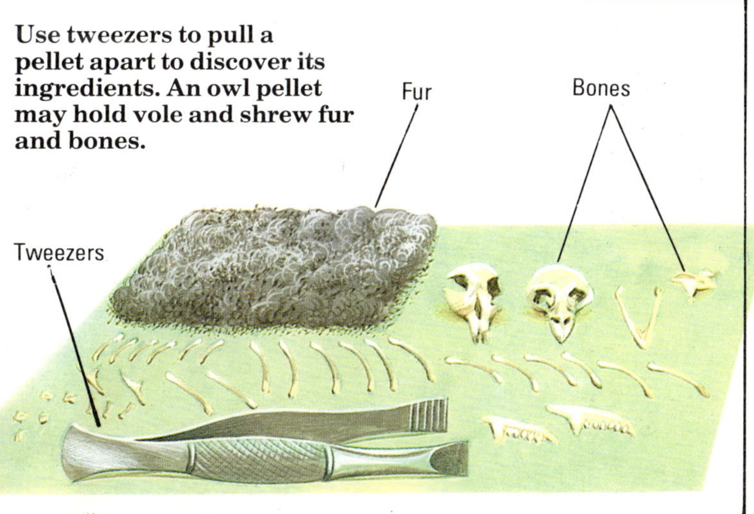

Flightless Birds

The birds we see around us find food or escape enemies by flying. But not all birds have wings strong enough to lift them into the air. These flightless birds must nest on the ground and feed there or in water. Most can run or swim fast enough to escape fierce flesh-eating mammals. A few flightless birds can only hide. These once needed no defence because they lived on lonely islands where they had no enemies and no one could reach them.

There used to be far more kinds of flightless bird than those that are alive today. Most living flightless birds are found on islands in the southern oceans.

Penguins

Penguins are easily the most plentiful flightless birds. Millions of these smart black and white seabirds live around the shores of southern continents and islands. On land they stand upright and waddle awkwardly. Some toboggan down snowy slopes on their bellies.

A thick layer of body fat and oily, close-packed feathers help penguins to stay warm in cold sea water.

In the sea a penguin swims head-forward, rather like a duck. But it uses its wings as flippers to row itself along. Penguins are streamlined like torpedoes. They swim and dive fast and gracefully as they hunt for food. Some penguins eat the small shrimp-like creatures called krill. Others eat squid, which are larger.

Penguins in their turn are hunted. Leopard seals often catch and kill Adélie penguins. But these can leap up to 2 metres out of the water to find safety.

Amazing Emperors

Emperor penguins are the largest living penguins. All nest on ice around Antarctica – the coldest continent on Earth. Even more surprisingly, each female emperor penguin lays her one egg as the long, dark, bitter winter of Antarctica is just starting. To hatch the egg the father keeps it warmly tucked inside a fold of skin that hangs down from his belly. He incubates the egg for weeks without a meal.

Emperor penguins warm and guard their chicks amid ice and snow. They feed them on fish stored inside the throat.

Strange Birds of Australasia

Australia, New Zealand and nearby islands are homes to three strange-looking flightless birds. These are the emu, cassowary and kiwi.

Emus

Australia's emu is the second largest bird alive. An emu stands as tall as a man and weighs as much as a woman. This big bird lacks tail quills and has tiny wings. Drooping grey-brown feathers cover it like a long, untidy, hairy rug.

Flocks of emus roam Australia's dry grasslands, eating berries, fruits and insects. A startled emu can run as fast as a horse.

Females lay eggs in nests below a tree or bush. But males incubate the eggs.

At least six kinds of emu were alive 15,000 years or so ago. But only one species survives today.

Cassowaries

Cassowaries look rather like emus with short legs. They have a bare, brightly coloured neck and head. A bony helmet on the forehead helps a cassowary push its way through tropical forest. Cassowaries live in north Australia and New Guinea.

An angry cassowary will kick a man and can even kill him with the sharp spike on its inner toe.

Kiwis

The three kinds of kiwi from New Zealand are as big as chickens. They have been called roly-poly birds, and seem all body, bill and feet. A kiwi has weak eyes, but nostrils at the tip of the beak help it to find worms. A kiwi lays a larger egg for its size than any other bird.

Winged Sprinters

We have just seen something of the flightless birds of Australasia. Other kinds live in South America and Africa. Scientists call the whole group *ratites*, from a Latin word for 'raft'. Ratites have a flat breastbone rather like a raft. Flying birds have a breastbone that juts down like a ship's keel. This bone anchors the muscles that work the wings. Because ratites do not fly they do not need a jutting breastbone.

The ostrich of Africa and the rhea of South America are both ratites. But in some ways these big flightless birds are not alike, and may be unrelated.

The Ostrich

The ostrich is the largest bird alive. A male would bang his head on the ceiling of most living rooms. One male is almost as heavy as two men of average weight.

Males are black with white wing and tail plumes and bare pink necks, thighs and legs. Females are slightly smaller than the males and more drably coloured.

Ostriches roam Africa's open grasslands in flocks of up to 50 birds. They eat plants and small animals. If danger appears they run away as fast as a horse. If an enemy attacks they kick hard enough to kill.

Each male has up to four 'wives'. Altogether these lay up to 40 eggs in one nest on the ground. Each huge egg could make an omelette for several families. Baby ostriches can run soon after

hatching. But they lie still if an enemy approaches. Ostriches can live 50 years.

An ostrich can outrun a lion. But the bird is too big and its wings are too weak to fly.

Rheas

Rheas are the largest birds of the Americas. But a rhea is far smaller than an ostrich. Rheas are shorter than most people and it would take six rheas to weigh as much as one male ostrich.

Unlike ostriches, rheas have feathered necks and thighs. But like ostriches they roam and run in flocks on open grassland. Their homelands are the pampas of southern South America.

Each male has five or six mates. Only the male sits on the eggs these lay. As many as 150 eggs were counted in one nest; 20 to 50 is usual.

Archaeopteryx

Lost Birds

Every bird we see came from the first birds, which lived 150 million years ago. In turn, these early birds sprang from ancestors that lived still earlier. The birds' first back-boned ancestors were fish. From fish came amphibians and reptiles. Birds arose from the so-called archosaurs or 'ruling reptiles'. This group also gave rise to the crocodiles and dinosaurs.

Are Birds Dinosaurs?
Some people think the first birds evolved from creatures like *Compsognathus*, a dinosaur no larger than a hen. Like birds, *Compsognathus* was probably warm blooded. The first birds also shared some of this dinosaur's other features. They had claws on their wings. Their beaks had teeth, and they had a long

Ichthyornis

tail like a reptile's. Even their feathers were really split and frayed scales.

'Ancient Wing'

Early birds walked, climbed trees, and glided down near lagoons. Some fell into the lagoons and drowned. But the soft mud preserved the marks left by their bones and feathers. Scientists call these early crow-sized birds *Archaeopteryx*: 'ancient wing'.

Archaeopteryx did not have the strong flight muscles of a modern flying bird. But these early birds gave rise to other kinds that flew very efficiently.

Archaeopteryx **may have spread its wings to trap prey.** *Hesperornis* **was a flightless diving bird.** *Ichthyornis* **looked much like a tern.**

Vanished Giants

The world's largest-ever land animals became extinct when dinosaurs died out 65 million years ago. In time mammals such as lions and elephants were to take their place. Meanwhile, big, powerful kinds of bird appeared. For a while it seemed giant birds might rule the land.

These birds were far too big to fly. But some were strong and fierce enough to fight off almost any enemy.

Fierce Flesh-Eaters

One huge bird was *Diatryma*. This creature stood taller than a man and had a large beak shaped like a parrot's. *Diatryma* may have used its beak to cut up plants, or possibly to tear up flesh.

Phororhacos was as big as *Diatryma* and maybe even fiercer. Its big beak was hooked like an eagle's. *Phororhacos* very likely killed and ate beasts as big as goats.

Both birds had long, strong legs and could have chased and run down their prey.

Gentle Grazers

While some giant prehistoric birds were as fierce as lions or tigers, others led peaceful lives like cows. Instead of eating flesh these flightless birds grazed, or browsed on shrubs and trees.

Flocks of giant grazing birds once roamed the island of Madagascar. Each of these elephant birds stood 3 metres tall and weighed more than six men. Stories of such birds gave rise to the legend of the roc, a bird whose spread wings darkened the sky.

One kind of prehistoric 'emu' from Australia stood as tall as the elephant bird and was probably a little heavier than that.

Tallest of all giant grazers was *Dinornis maximus*, whose name means 'greatest of the terrible birds'. This monster from New Zealand had legs like a cart horse's. It stood nearly a metre taller than the elephant bird but was only half its weight.

Prehistoric Penguins

About 30 million years ago giant penguins swam in southern oceans. Their fossil bones show that at least two species stood tall enough to reach a man's shoulder. Other big, flightless seabirds swam in northern oceans.

In time, most flightless giant birds were killed off by their mammal rivals.

Phororhacos **(top) flourished in South America 20 million years ago.** *Diatryma* **lived in North America 50 million years ago.**

Birds Destroyed by Man

Probably more kinds of bird have been killed off by man than by any other mammal. Most of these lost birds vanished in the last 600 years or so.

Birds That Could Not Fly

Man's first victims were birds that ran or swam but could not fly. Most had lived safely enough on lonely islands until hunters and settlers arrived. Then people began to kill the birds for meat. With settlers came cats, dogs, rats and goats. These ate or trampled on the chicks and eggs of flightless birds that nested on the ground.

Below: Dodos were first found on the lonely island of Mauritius in 1598. Within a century man had killed off these big, flightless birds.

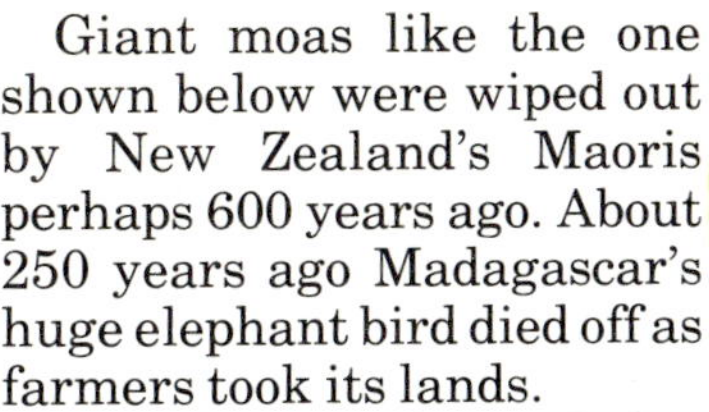

Giant moas like the one shown below were wiped out by New Zealand's Maoris perhaps 600 years ago. About 250 years ago Madagascar's huge elephant bird died off as farmers took its lands.

The great auk was a flightless northern seabird like a penguin. Sailors killed millions. This made great auks rare and valuable. In 1844 collectors killed and stuffed the last few left.

Giant moa

Pigeons and Parakeets

In North America early in the 1800s migrating flocks of passenger pigeons darkened the sky for hours. Maybe no other kind of bird was so plentiful. Yet by 1915 farmers and hunters had killed it off. In the same way the Carolina parakeet died out in the 1920s.

In the last 300 years man has probably destroyed 10 times more kinds of bird than those that became extinct for other reasons.

Birds at Risk

Since birds began, two million species may have lived at one time or another. But no more than 12,000 kinds probably ever lived at the same time. Of the 9000 kinds of bird alive today a growing number are at risk of dying out because of man and his activities.

Hunters slaughter birds for meat, feathers, or just for fun. Each year thousands of songbirds are shot or trapped migrating between Europe and Africa. Then, too, some kinds of bird are growing scarcer because so many have been caught and kept alone in cages where they cannot breed. Some also have unsuitable breeding conditions.

Other species suffer where man clears wild land so as to make farms or cities. If he fells forests he robs woodland birds of homes. If he drains swamps, water birds lose feeding grounds.

Man also poisons birds, by accident. Oil spilt in the sea can choke seabirds to death. Pesticides that kill insects have harmed birds which ate animals that fed upon the poisoned insects.

Above: North America's ivory-billed woodpecker may already be extinct.

Left: Only three dozen or so California condors still nest in the wild.

Introduced Enemies

On oceanic islands animals brought in by man threaten certain birds. Cats and dogs are threatening the rare kagu of New Caledonia, and the Hawaiian duck. Stoats from Europe kill many of New Zealand's big, flightless parrots called kakapos. In Jamaica mongooses have almost wiped out a tree duck.

About to Perish

A few kinds of bird have become so rare that they seem certain to vanish altogether. Such species include the Kauai o-o from Hawaii. By 1980 fewer than 10 of these honeyeaters survived. By the time you read these words there may be none.

Above: No more than 10 Japanese crested ibises lived on into the 1980s.

Saved from Extinction

People who care about birds are trying hard to save the species most in danger.

Governments set aside areas of wetland, forest, heath and so on as nature reserves where birds are safe from interference.

Rare birds are caught and bred in zoos. The Hawaiian goose was saved like this. Several other species may be rescued like this, too.

Below: A few hundred Audouin's gulls survive on Mediterranean islands.

Surprising Facts

Spine-tailed swift

Record Holders

A few people run faster or live longer than other people, or can perform some feat that seems amazing.

In the same way, certain birds can outfly, outlive or in some way outdo almost all the other bird species. On these pages we look at a few of these record holders.

Speedy Swifts

Probably no bird flies faster than one kind of spine-tailed swift that lives in Asia. Slim, fast-beating, scythe-shaped wings speed this small creature through the air around it at more than 170 km/h.

A racing pigeon has flown slightly faster than that. But a wind blowing at over 96 km/h helped it along. In fact it was moving only 80 km/h faster than the air surrounding it.

Some people say spine-tailed swifts can exceed 350 km/h – twice as fast as their official record.

Whooper swans

High Fliers

High up, the thin, cold air makes flying difficult. No bird is known to fly as high as Mt Everest, the highest peak. But climbers have seen Alpine choughs and eagles far up on that mountain's slopes.

Certain birds probably fly even higher on migration. In 1967 a plane and an Irish radar station reported whooper swans near Scotland at 8200 metres up.

Long Lives

Small birds die young of hunger, disease or enemy attack. Most robins, great tits and starlings fail to reach their third birthday.

Big birds live longer. Many herring gulls live to about 20, and royal albatrosses often live to 33. Big birds fed and cared for in zoos live longest of all. One Andean condor kept in Moscow Zoo reached the ripe old age of at least 72.

Friends and Foes of Man

Birds are surprisingly important in our lives. We eat some birds and their eggs. People collect thick layers of seabird droppings for fertilizing soil.

But certain birds are pests that damage crops.

Feathered Thieves

Where man grows certain types of plant, the birds that eat them multiply.

Where farms grow grain, sparrows or their relatives are plentiful. Around the world millions of house sparrows steal countless tonnes of wheat each year from fields or storage bins. In much of Africa, the worst enemies of farmers are the sparrow's relatives called queleas. In a year, farmers kill about 1000 million of these seed-eaters. But 9000 million more survive. Queleas are probably more plentiful than wild birds of any other species on Earth.

Queleas belong to the weaver birds, so called for the way in which they build their nests.

These three pictures show how a male quelea weaves its nest in a tree or between reeds.

Above: It can take less than two months to grow a hatchling into a big broiler chicken.

Below: One tree may hold 400 quelea nests. Farmers use flame throwers on large colonies.

Living Larders

Farmers have kept hens, ducks, geese and other birds for food for thousands of years. Chickens are descended from the wild jungle fowl of southern Asia. Turkeys were first tamed by the American Indians.

Turkeys are the meatiest domesticated birds. The largest known turkey was half as heavy as a man.

But in one year chickens lay more eggs than turkeys. One hen laid 361 eggs – almost one each day. This helps to explain why the world's farmers keep so many chickens. There is one chicken for every human being on Earth.

Bird Mimics

Magpie

Of all animals only certain birds can imitate a human voice. These birds can also copy other sounds. The best bird mimics are so good that people often cannot tell the real sound from its imitation.

Crow Copycats
Jackdaws, magpies and some other crows are among the best mimics.

As a boy, the British naturalist Gerald Durrell kept two magpies. These birds made piping and hiccuping sounds like those used by a maid when she called the hens at feeding time. The hens would run up to the magpies, who screeched at them wickedly.

Starlings
The starling family also has splendid mimics. The common starling can imitate various birdsongs and a woodpecker's laughing cry.

Hill mynahs are glossy black starlings with yellow flaps of skin on the head. They learn to whistle short tunes, chuckle, cough, and speak more plainly than any other talking bird.

Mockingbirds
The 31 kinds of mockingbird, catbird and thrasher are thrush-like birds of America. Many of them are fine mimics.

One mockingbird was said

to mix 30 other songs with its own burbling melody. Florida's mockingbirds soon learnt the exact songs of caged nightingales brought from Europe. Special tests showed they even imitated bits of song the human ear could not detect.

A squeaky cartwheel and a postman's whistle are among the many sounds a mockingbird can manage.

Parrots

The most famous of all talking birds are some members of the parrot family. Wild parrots squawk or shriek. Only tame ones copy other sounds. Perhaps they find it helps to stop them getting bored. Some parrots will sidle up and listen hard if you whistle or speak to them. Afterwards you may hear them trying out the new sounds they have just heard.

Some parrots learn to say more words than others. The little budgerigars include some splendid talkers. Cockatoos and macaws manage one or two phrases. Yellow-headed Amazon parrots are the best American talkers. But the world champion was an African grey parrot that spoke almost 1000 words.

A parrot like this one has learnt more words than any other bird.

Strange Behaviour

Egyptian vulture

Scientists studying how birds behave have had many surprises. They have found a few birds that hibernate and a few that use tools. Even the birds that we see around us sometimes behave in remarkable ways.

Tool-Users

The Egyptian vulture shown above drops stones on ostrich eggs to break their thick, hard shells. Then the bird eats the food inside.

Song thrushes also use stones as tools. A thrush breaks a snail shell by beating it against a stone.

Lammergeiers fly high and drop bones to smash them on rocks below. An old story says that a lammergeier once dropped a tortoise that hit and killed a famous Greek thinker.

The Galápagos finch grips a twig in its beak to catch insects hiding in holes in the wood of dead trees.

Crazy Crows

If a male crow sees his reflection in a window he may think he is seeing a rival male and attack. One crow beat against one window day after day for a week. The bird flew at the glass so hard that he made himself bleed. Attacks like this usually happen only during the breeding season.

Feeding the Fish

A famous photograph shows a bird feeding fish. The bird was a cardinal, an American songbird. The fish were goldfish. The place was the edge of a pond. The bird mistook the open mouths of the goldfish for the gaping beaks of its chicks.

Crows sometimes attack their reflections in mistake for other crows.

The Sleeping One

People once thought that swallows slept through the winter, underground. Now we know they migrate. But at least one bird hibernates. This is Nuttall's poorwill, a North American nightjar. In winter, it hides in a crevice, grows cold, and so uses up energy 30 times more slowly than usual. This helps it live for months without food.

A hibernating poorwill seems to stop breathing and its heartbeat grows too faint to be felt.

Winged Invaders

Wild birds at home in one continent sometimes invade another. A few kinds fly there freely. Caged birds travel by ship or plane but may escape or be freed. If food is plentiful the birds thrive and breed.

Cattle Egrets
These long-legged birds mainly live in Africa, southern Europe and Asia. But about 1930, some flew or were blown by gales from Africa to South America. There they fed on insects stirred up by the hooves of cattle, just as they used to feed when in Africa.

The egrets multiplied and spread north and west. By 1950 they reached Florida in the USA. By 1958 they had entered Colombia.

Meanwhile others spread south-east from Asia and reached Australia.

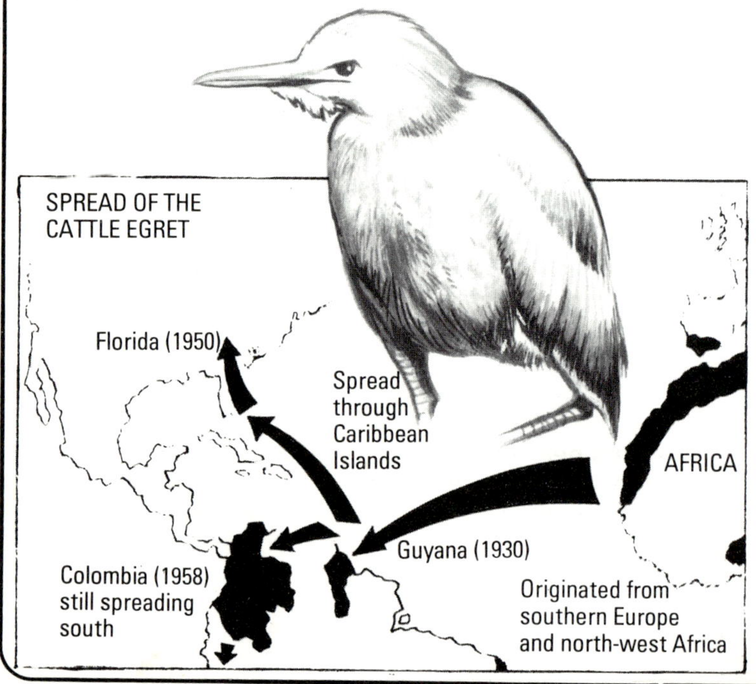

A parakeet near London. These tropical birds have managed to breed in cool, cloudy England.

Ring-Necked Parakeets

Ring-necked parakeets live in the warm countries of Africa and south Asia. There, these handsome green parrots fly in flocks and feed on fruit and grain.

In 1969, Londoners were amazed to see small flocks of parakeets near England's largest city. Since then the birds have become a familiar sight in at least some London suburbs. The invaders may have come from free-flying colonies that escaped from gardens.

Birds from Home

In the 1800s settlers from Europe freed many European birds in parts of the world far from their homelands.

In 1890, 100 starlings were released in New York City. They bred and spread. Now millions live in the USA and southern Canada. In the same way, starlings invaded Australia, New Zealand and South Africa.

Starlings eat fruit and mess up buildings. Like sparrows – also spread by man – they can be pests.

Pirates and Parasites

Frigatebirds

Finding food, building nests and raising chicks take up much of most birds' lives. But a few dodge hard work. Bird pirates steal food or nests from other birds. Bird parasites leave their eggs for others to hatch.

Aerial Raiders

Frigatebirds are large, slim-winged seabirds of the tropics. At breeding time, males attract females by blowing up big brightly coloured flaps of skin. At this time of the year they also earn their other name of the man o' war bird. Frigatebirds swoop down on boobies, terns and tropic birds as these fly inshore to bring food to their young.

A frigatebird pecks at a victim's wings and tail until it drops a beakful of fish. The frigatebird snaps up the fish and flies off.

Great skuas are big, brown gull-like birds. They knock flying gannets off balance to make them cough up food. They also steal penguin eggs and chicks.

Skuas and frigatebirds also catch their own fish.

Squatters

House sparrows sometimes steal house-martins' nests. The sparrows wait until the nests have been built. Then they drive the owners away.

The martins may return and throw out the invaders. But their weak beaks are usually no match for sparrows' thick, strong beaks.

Cuckoo's egg

Meadow pipit's egg

A cuckoo tends to lay eggs of the same colour as those of the bird whose nest it uses.

Uncaring Parents

In spring a female cuckoo will lay one egg in each of several nests of a smaller kind of bird. Meadow pipits and hedge sparrows are the usual victims. They hatch a cuckoo's egg with their own eggs. Then the cuckoo chick throws out the other chicks and so gets all the food its foster parents bring.

Cowbirds, drongo-cuckoos and parasitic flycatchers also lay their eggs in the nests of other species.

A great skua threatens a petrel on its nest. Skuas steal much of their food from other birds.

Unbelievable Birds

Certain birds are designed in an almost unbelievable way. Their special designs may help these birds find food or escape enemies in a manner that other birds find impossible. What seems to us strange or awkward may ensure the birds' survival.

Birds Like Bats
The oilbirds of northern South America look like ordinary birds but fly in pitch darkness, like bats. They steer by making clicks and listening to the echoes bounced back from the walls of the caves where they roost. Some sleep as much as one kilometre below ground.

Skimmers use the long half of their beak to scoop up fish.

Skimmers
Skimmers look like big terns. But the lower half of a skimmer's beak is far longer and larger than the upper half. To catch fish the bird flies along with the lower half of its beak ploughing through the water. When this part of its beak touches a fish, the skimmer snaps its beak shut and raises the fish into the air. No other bird has such a widely gaping beak.

One kind of skimmer lives in the Americas; another in Africa; a third in Asia.

A Living Fossil?

The first known bird looked rather like a reptile. *Archaeopteryx* was a prehistoric bird with teeth, a long, bony tail, and claws on its wings. In time most birds lost all these things. One bird still looks like this when young.

The hoatzin chicks have clawed wings that help them climb, in the same way that claws helped *Archaeopteryx* 150 million years ago. As they grow, hoatzins lose their claws, but still climb with their wings. These strange birds live in South America.

Myths and Monstrosities

Before scientists studied birds people believed strange tales about them. They even believed in birds that had never lived at all.

Feathered Fakes
Skilful craftsmen often 'invented' a new species of bird. They took pieces from dead birds of several kinds and joined the bits together. Some made fake birds for a joke. Some sold their fakes for large sums to collectors of strange and rare things.

A hundred years ago one fake made from a drongo and a cuckoo-shrike deceived a bird expert: he called it the first known example of a kind of thrush-like bird.

A bare-fronted hoodwink: made from a crow, duck, plover and red wax.

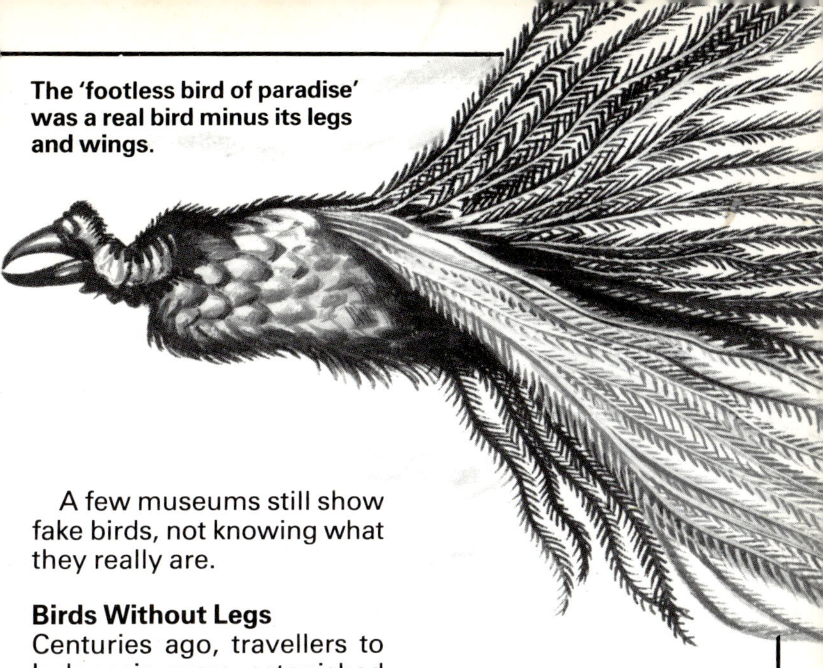

The 'footless bird of paradise' was a real bird minus its legs and wings.

A few museums still show fake birds, not knowing what they really are.

Birds Without Legs

Centuries ago, travellers to Indonesia were astonished to find traders selling the skins of birds with long, lovely feathers, and yet no wings or legs. Legend said that they came from heaven.

In the 1700s this led the famous Swedish naturalist Karl Linnaeus to call one a 'footless bird of paradise'.

In the 1820s a Frenchman learnt that the birds really came from New Guinea. He found that the people there removed the wings and legs before selling the skins.

This discovery killed the legend of a bird without feet. But real birds of the kind that gave rise to the legend are still called birds of paradise.

Bird or Fish?

Barnacle geese owe their name to an old belief about how they started life. People thought they came from goose barnacles. These relatives of crabs have feathery 'feet' poking from a shell on a long stalk curved like a goose's neck and growing from a piece of driftwood. People finding goose barnacles washed up on the shore believed these were young geese.

Some Roman Catholics argued this meant that geese were fish. So they ate geese on Fridays when eating fowl or flesh was not allowed.

INDEX

Page numbers in *italics* refer to illustrations.